Isle of Man Classic Steam

The Isle of Man Railway in colour from the 1950s to the Ailsa era

Robert Robotham

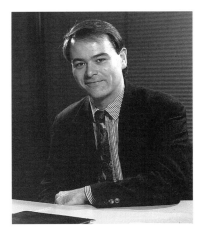

As with all railways, it is the people that operate them, often in adverse conditions, that are the real unsung heroes.
This book is warmly dedicated to all those who have run the IOMR and is offered as an inspiration to those who run the preserved Douglas to Port Erin section.
May it continue to flourish and maybe one day serve Peel again!

Robert Robotham was born in Nottingham and first became interested in railways by watching the inspirational performance of the famous Annesley to Woodward 'Runners' on the Great Central main line near Wilford. Although primarily a Great Central enthusiast, his interests extend to the Somerset and Dorset, the Waverley route, the County Donegal Railways and the Isle of Man Railway. He is already well known as the author of such Ian Allan books as *On Great Central Lines* and *On West Highland Lines* and, in the autumn, will be the author of another full colour album by Colourpoint, *Last Days of the Wee Donegal*.

In addition to his interest in railways, Robert Robotham is a member of the Territorial Army and works for Racal Communications in the railway sector, running a team dedicated to the needs of Railtrack.

6 5 4 3 2 1

© Robert Robotham
Newtownards 1998

Designed by Colourpoint Books, Newtownards
Maps drawn by Barry Craig for Colourpoint
Printed by ColourBooks

ISBN 1 898392 43 9

Colourpoint Books
Unit D5, Ards Business Centre
Jubilee Road
NEWTOWNARDS
County Down
Northern Ireland
BT23 4YH
Tel: (01247) 820505/819787 Ex 239
Fax: (01247) 821900
E-mail: info@colourpoint.co.uk
Web-site: www.colourpoint.co.uk

Front photograph: No 14 *Thornhill* makes a vigorous departure from Douglas with the 3.45 pm to Ramsey on 20 April 1957.

Frontispiece: No 10 *G H Wood* runs along the superb western coastline at Lady Port with the 10.47 am St John's to Ramsey on 3 June 1968. The locomotive sports its new coat of Ailsa green paint. On this section the flat bottom rails that were normally spiked directly into the sleepers, were placed in chairs and helped stop the rails from spreading – the 'Cale' being a particular culprit. A speed restriction of 12 mph was imposed here, the norm being 40 mph.

Back photograph: No 8 *Fenella* waits to depart from St John's with a Douglas service in September 1964.

CONTENTS

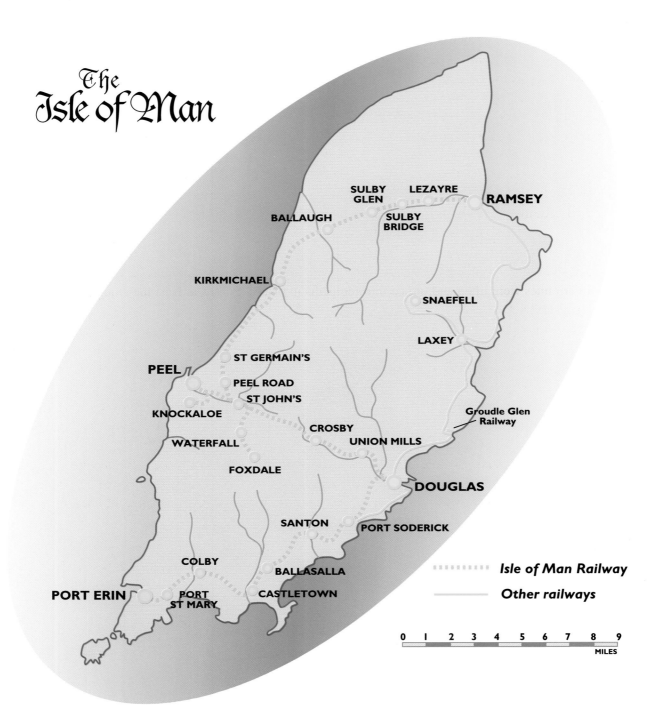

The Isle of Man

SULBY GLEN
LEZAYRE
RAMSEY
BALLAUGH
SULBY BRIDGE
KIRKMICHAEL
SNAEFELL
LAXEY
ST GERMAIN'S
PEEL
PEEL ROAD
ST JOHN'S
KNOCKALOE
Groudle Glen Railway
CROSBY
UNION MILLS
WATERFALL
FOXDALE
DOUGLAS
SANTON
PORT SODERICK
COLBY
BALLASALLA
PORT ERIN
PORT ST MARY
CASTLETOWN

.... Isle of Man Railway
——— Other railways

0 1 2 3 4 5 6 7 8 9
MILES

INTRODUCTION

The Isle of Man Railway has to be one of the great survivors of all the narrow gauge railways in the British Isles — even if only in part. It opened from Douglas to Peel, via St John's, as long ago as 1 July 1873, with Douglas to Port Erin opening on 1 August 1874 and the Manx Northern line from Ramsey to St John's on 23 September 1879. It served the Island population virtually constantly (including playing a key role in both world wars) until 1965/6, when repair costs looked so great that they could have forced permanent closure. Passenger traffic had fallen, due to the advent of motor-bus services, increased car ownership amongst the Island population and a drift of lucrative tourists away from the Island in summer, to explore warmer climes, tempted by cheap package deals to Spain and the Mediterranean.

However, it was saved by a benefactor, the Marquis of Ailsa, who spent £43,000 of his own money to restore services the following year, taking over on 3 April 1967. Train services started on 3 June. Unfortunately, even he ran into financial difficulty and the northern routes never re-opened after the 1968 season.

Today, interest in the railway has never been better and one wonders about the rapidity with which the northern lines were lifted and turned into footpaths in places. Surely, at least the Douglas to Peel line could have survived.

Space does not permit a detailed historical account of the steam railway, the aim of this book being to show the lines in the 1950s and 1960s through a selection of colour photographs. However, readers will find J I C Boyd's three volumes on the *The Isle of Man Railway* required reading, as is *The Manx Northern Railway* by R Preston Hendry & R Powell Hendry. Ivo Peters filmed the line in this period and his work is now available on video. Even better, the Douglas to Port Erin line is still open so, unlike the Somerset and Dorset, a trip behind an 1870s vintage locomotive can still be made today. *The Isle of Man Steam Railway*, by Barry Edwards, is also an excellent volume.

The discovery of some excellent transparencies taken in the 1950s and 1960s prompted me to engage in this work. They capture the atmosphere of the line totally — one which is re-created by the Douglas to Port Erin survivor today. Many thanks are due to Ron White for his help and advice during the preparation of this book.

Robert Robotham, Sherborne, June 1998.

Construction and Opening

Proposals to construct a railway on the Isle of Man go back to 1845. Nothing materialised until a census taken in 1864, which indicated the desire for a railway to link together the population of the Island for both freight and passenger business. On 21 April 1870, key Manx businessmen met in Douglas to discuss the establishment of such a scheme. They focused on building lines from Douglas to Castletown (the Island capital until 1866), with future extensions to Port St Mary and Port Erin, and Douglas to Peel and Ramsey. The company was registered on 19 December 1870 as The Isle of Man Railway Company Ltd and had a share capital of some £200,000. By the end of 1871, only £30,000 had been pledged, which led to the Ramsey line being abandoned and concentration on the Peel route, together with a more centralised station next to the harbour. The gauge was to be 3'0" and the engineer appointed was Henry Vignoles.

Lack of financial support led to help being sought from the mainland and this came from The Duke of Sutherland, a railway enthusiast and financier, and Mr John Pender MP, (later Sir John Pender), the railway financier. The Duke was Chairman of the Company from 14 November 1872, for seven years. Mr Pender, who joined on 1 May 1872, took over the Chairman's post, after the Duke, and held it for seventeen years.

This renewed impetus saw the Douglas to Peel line opening on 1 July 1873, the 11½ miles having been constructed on easy grades for most of its distance by contractors Watson and Smith. Three 2-4-0T locomotives in green livery had been supplied by Beyer Peacock, and No 1, appropriately named *Sutherland*, had pulled a special train which consisted of four wagons fitted with seats, on 1 May. It promptly derailed at Peel and the train had to be rescued by the building contractor's locomotive *Mona*, which returned it to Douglas. It was not until 27 June that a fifteen coach train ran (twenty-nine six-wheelers had been supplied by the Metropolitan Railway Carriage and Wagon Company) and, following this, formal opening took place on 1 July 1873. The first official train carried the proud banner, 'Douglas and Peel United', complete with the band of the Royal Bengal Fusiliers playing from an open wagon.

On 1 August 1874, the Douglas to Port Erin line opened. It was built by Irish and Welsh workers and was not without its difficulties when the main contractor withdrew, just before completion in June. This 15½ mile route was more steeply graded than the Peel line and required heavier trains to be banked out of Douglas. Locomotives 4 and 5 arrived in 1874, with more coaches, especially for the Port Erin service. The line was an instant success and it was quickly realised that more passing loops would have to be laid in to cope with the demand for train services. Passenger traffic was supplemented by a Post Office contract for the carriage of mails to both Peel and Port Erin.

The Manx Northern

Ramsey was still left without a railway and, as a result, a separate company, known as the Manx Northern Railway was registered on 17 March 1878. Tynwald granted its consent on 1 January 1878, the line starting from St John's at a station within close proximity to the existing IOMR station on the Douglas to Peel line. It was built by J & W Grainger of Glasgow and Brebner and Fleming of Edinburgh, running along the coast through difficult country and necessitating two viaducts — at Glen Mooar and Glen Wyllin. The line ran via Peel Road, St Germain's, Kirkmichael, Ballaugh, Sulby Bridge and Lezayre to Ramsey and its harbour. This harbour was important to the MNR for the trans-shipment of goods to and from the mainland. Two locomotives were delivered from Sharp Stewart and became No 1 *Ramsey* and No 2 *Northern*. These locomotives were soon found to be underpowered and No 3 *Thornhill* was ordered from Beyer Peacock, being of the same design as the IOMR locomotives.

The line opened on 23 September 1879 and, curiously, was operated, under an agreement, by the Isle of Man Railway but maintained and administered by the MNR itself. After a honeymoon period, relations became strained (free passes for directors were withdrawn between the railways) and there were disagreements over timetabling and the connectional arrangements at St John's. To make matters worse, in 1882 MNR coaching stock was banned from the IOMR, due to a derailment at Union Mills.

Foxdale

Then, in 1886, a short 2½ mile line opened from St John's to Foxdale (The Foxdale Railway Company). The Foxdale line was leased to the MNR for fifty years and, in return, the MNR provided the rolling stock for half the revenue. The line was constructed primarily to serve the lead mines at Foxdale, lead being sent to Ramsey quay for trans-shipment and the return traffic of coal from the mainland for the mines' use. Opened on 16/17 August, the line climbed at a gradient of 1:49 through Waterfall halt to Upper Foxdale. However, the lead mines were already in decline and the line was in financial trouble virtually immediately. Dumbells Bank announced that they intended to recover debts incurred and, consequently, the Foxdale company put pressure on the MNR to pay unpaid lease payments. What freight there was, was worked mainly by No 4 *Caledonia*, which arrived for the purpose in 1885. The MNR hoped that the Foxdale line would be extended to Castletown or Ballasalla and link up with the IOMR. But, by 1891, the Foxdale company went into liquidation, leaving the MNR to operate the line under the fifty year lease terms.

Competition & Takeovers

During this period the MNR and IOMR faced a threat from the projected building of an east coast route from Douglas to Ramsey by the Douglas, Laxey and Ramsey Railway Company. This did not materialise in totality until 1899 and was known as the Douglas and Laxey Coast Electric Tramway. A branch up Snaefell had opened from 1895. Other actual competition did come, from a short lived steamer service.

The IOMR was fearful of this competition and, when the tramway announced it was interested in taking over the MNR in 1898, it also made a bid. The MNR also offered itself to the IOMR for £72,500, but this was declined.

The collapse of Dumbells Bank in 1900 had little effect on the IOMR but the coastal tramway went into liquidation. The MNR had little option but to offer itself for sale to the IOMR, but at a reduced price of £60,000. Again, this offer was rejected, as the IOMR itself had designs on the tramway.

However, following a 1903 Tynwald investigation it was decided that, due to the perilous state of the MNR and the associated Foxdale company, both should be taken over by the IOMR. The Isle of Man Railways Act of 24 May 1905 allowed this, for a cost of £67,500. Much repair work was carried out on the infrastructure between Ramsey and St John's, especially on the two viaducts. This allowed an express service to be introduced between Ramsey and Douglas to compete with the tramway and its more direct route. However, in 1911 the Foxdale mines closed, leaving a sparse passenger service with the Foxdale coach (now IOMR No F39).

World War One

The outbreak of World War One in 1914 seriously affected holiday traffic from the mainland, which virtually ceased after the 1914 season (it had topped the one million passengers mark in 1913). The Isle of Man was used for interning prisoners of war and other aliens, a camp being constructed at Knockaloe, near Peel, which was soon linked by a railway. The traffic to and from the camp was considerable and, despite the war, three quarters of a million people were carried on the network in 1916. Due to the steep gradient of the Knockaloe line, MNR locomotive No 4 *Caledonia*, an 0-6-0T, worked the line. To allow transfer of goods to Knockaloe, an extension from Peel station to the harbour was laid in. At night, a locomotive was always kept in steam at Ramsey to move troops from the garrison, should an emergency arrive. Amazingly, by 1917, passenger numbers were back over the million mark and freight, both war and general goods and livestock, was on the increase.

Above: In 1961 the IOMR purchased two railcars from the County Donegal Railway. These retained their County Donegal numbers. Here railcars Nos 19 and 20 (nearest the camera) await to depart from Braddan for Douglas, having run a special for one of the open air church services on 2 August 1964.

The CDR had turntables at each terminus and ran the railcars as single units. The IOMR did not possess turntables for turning the railcars, so instead they ran back to back with the one pulling the other — in this case No 19 will be pulling No 20.

D J Mitchell / ColourRail

Below: Railcars 19 (leading) and 20 arrive in the loop at Union Mills in August 1967 with a train from Peel to Douglas. The County Donegal railcar livery was 'geranium red' lower body panels and cream upper panels and roof. The two cars had differently painted front ends — No 19 having a small triangular pattern on the radiator whilst on No 20 the cream band curved gracefully to a point below the radiator. These features were retained by the Isle of Man Railway, the only changes being that the roof and upper body panels were painted red and that the red was of a much deeper hue.

ColourRail

Above: No 10, *G H Wood* runs through St Germain's with a Ramsey to Douglas service in 1968. The track looks as though it could do with some maintenance, but there was little money available for this expenditure. Indeed it was this lack of investment, and the resulting backlog, that stored up future problems as the Marquis of Ailsa was unable to afford any capital investment to renew such assets as track.

D J Mitchell / ColourRail

Below: No 8, *Fenella* passes over Glen Mooar viaduct with a Ramsey service in July 1961. The structure was of wrought iron lattice girders that were supported by two stone piers to a height of 75 feet. It was strengthened in 1914 and totally reconstructed in 1921.

ColourRail

The Inter-War Years

The end of the war brought the eight hour working day and thus less flexibility of railway workers. The motor lorry had been advanced by the war and so too had the charabanc. However, post-war, the holiday traffic returned, Douglas station being enlarged between 1922 and 1925. 1925 saw the high point of 1,344,620 passengers carried. From 1926, numbers declined and the new Managing Director, Mr A H Teare, encountered the first real competition to the railways in the Isle of Man with the arrival of the *Manxland Bus Company*. The railway's response was typically bullish. Train service frequencies were increased and special offer fares introduced. These were 'rover' tickets, which cost only 5 shillings for two days or 10 shillings for a week. The IOMR even associated itself with the buses and joined with some local operators as *Manx Motors*. However, the railway then obtained their own buses as a separate division. Other bus operators went under and two were brought out by the railway and renamed *Isle of Man Road Services Ltd*. Despite the competition, passenger numbers levelled out at three-quarters of a million, the railway remaining in profit.

An innovative idea in 1935 was the purchase of Glen Wyllin, on the Ramsey line, which was linked by a footpath to the railway. The Glen was developed with a boating lake, various amusements and concert facilities. Express services were reintroduced on the Douglas to Ramsey line in 1937, taking only one hour, with limited stops at St John's and Kirkmichael.

World War Two

World War Two saw another sharp fall back in holiday business but, to compensate, the forces opened training camps, bringing an influx of service personnel. Also, the Island became a place for 'aliens' and the railway helped to transport them (some 3,500) to Port Erin. The RAF had personnel at Jurby and Andreas. Ronaldsway was a Fleet Air Arm base. Waterfall, on the Foxdale branch, was used as a trans-shipment point for troops on night exercises. A special timetable was introduced to cope with all this, with late night trains and connections with shipping services. Even Foxdale's mines were used, to provide construction material for airfields, and this meant a considerable number of freight trains. As well as all this, bus services were cut back and motor car usage reduced, due to petrol rationing, which saw the local population making greater use of the railway. At the end of the war, some 14,000 trains had run for the Services.

Post War Rise and Decline

Following the war tourism resurged upon the Island and the timetable reflected this, with eight trains per day from Douglas to Peel and Ramsey and eleven to Port Erin. Over one million journeys were recorded in 1950, up by some 300,000 on the immediate pre-war years. A refurbishment plan for locomotives, rolling stock and infrastructure began but prices had risen significantly and, to save costs, locomotive cannibalism took place, with No 7 being the first, followed by No 2. New boilers were needed for three of the others.

As with railways on the mainland, the spread of the motor car and bus saw a downward spiral in numbers of passengers and freight tonnage carried. Firstly, car ownership increased significantly, both amongst the Island population and visitors. Secondly, the arrival of larger numbers of buses had a major impact. Sunday trains to Peel and Ramsey were withdrawn, although they lasted to Port Erin until 1956. This helped reduce the amount of overtime paid to staff. Winter services were also reduced and, by 1959, services were operated on a 8.30am to 6.30pm basis. By the early 1960s, winter services were minimal — Peel to St John's being closed to passengers in the winter of 1960-1. The following winter, the entire system was operated with only one engine a day in steam, with the Ramsey service closed and substituted by a bus. Douglas to Port Erin fared better, with two trains per day. This decline did little to attract business and the 1962-3 winter had an even sparser service, with only one return train from Douglas to Port Erin, as well as the reduced Peel service and bus to Ramsey. This allowed operations with only one engine in steam, but did not allow decent return journeys for passengers.

In 1961, two railcars, purchased from the closed County Donegal Railways Joint Committee, arrived on 7 May. After refurbishment, they were put to use in 1961-2 on the Peel route. They struggled to cope with the gradients on the Port Erin line, although they were fitted with sanders. To economise further, the IOMR tried to purchase former CIE narrow gauge diesel locomotives, an offer which was declined. Frustratingly, they remained unsold.

Summer services still operated on all routes and there were occasional specials. Her Majesty, Queen Elizabeth The Queen Mother, travelled to Kirk Bradden from Douglas on 7 July 1963 on a special train hauled by No 11 *Maitland*. A new halt to serve the recently opened Curraghs Wildlife Park, between Sulby Glen and Ballaugh, did not bring any significant increase in traffic to the Ramsey line. By 1965, the railway was at crisis point and a trading loss of £8000 was recorded. Track was in dire need of repair and it was decided to close the railway on 13 November to effect them. The repairs were subsequently cancelled and no passenger services at all were operated in 1966. However, the 1966 TT races did see the County Donegal railcars act as a hospital train for potential casualties and the railway suffered the indignity of having St John's station used as a car park for Tynwald Day — an event that, ironically, had usually brought many travellers by rail in previous years.

The Ailsa Era and Beyond

The Tynwald Transport Review recommended that the Douglas to Peel line should be retained as a tourist attraction. Meetings were held on the future of the railway and the Isle of Man Railway Supporters' Association formed. The Marquis of Ailsa agreed to assist and took on a lease of twenty-one years, with an option to suspend services after just five.

On 3 June 1967, the whole railway (except the Foxdale branch) re-opened and *Maitland* pulled the re-opening special to Peel. Four more trains followed and all locomotives were painted in the now famous 'Ailsa Green'.

The service was aimed at the tourist market and, in 1968, services were again reduced to cut costs. The service ended before the intended end of the timetable, this being 6 September from Ramsey and from Peel on the 7th. No one knew it then, but the northern lines were never to re-open. For 1969 only the Port Erin line ran, with financial support, as The Isle of Man Victorian Steam Railway Company Ltd. In 1971 the Marquis decided to withdraw from the lease. From then on, the railway was operated by the railway company, which operated the Port Erin line with assistance from the Tourist Board. Centenary celebrations took place on the Port Erin line in 1974.

However (and disastrously), at the end of 1973 the Peel, Ramsey and Foxdale lines were sold for scrap, for only £149,000, to Millen Metals of Belfast. Some rail was re-used and abandoned coaches sold. Unbelievably, a Tynwald Committee recommended that no more grants be paid to the railway and claimed that closure would not affect tourism. However, in 1975, a grant allowed services to operate, though only from Port Erin to Castletown (and only Sunday to Fridays). In 1976 services ran to Ballasalla, and by 1977 they were back at Douglas. On 1 September 1976, Isle of Man National Transport had been formed to run bus services, taking over the railway's responsibility for them.

In more recent times, more cost savings have been made, notably rationalisation at Douglas and the unfortunate demolition of the canopies and semaphore signalling. With a smaller railway to operate, some locomotives were taken out of service. Today, the railway's future is secure following Tynwald approving purchase, following the 1976 General Election. Together with The Manx Electric, it operates under the banner of 'Isle of Man Railways'. The railway's official guide is currently the best way of learning of recent history.

The following photographs show the railway in the 1950s and 1960s, when the complete system still operated. I hope they encourage readers to visit the railway and experience it for themselves, as well as offering inspiration to those who are involved with the restoration and operation of the line today.

Above: The next viaduct on the Ramsey line after Glen Mooar was at Glen Wyllin which was also totally rebuilt, this time in 1915. No 12 *Hutchinson* crosses Glen Wyllin viaduct with a Douglas bound train in July 1961. Glen Wyllin was acquired by the railway in 1935 to be developed as an activity destination for holiday makers, a boating lake and other sporting facilities, such as golf, being provided. A path linked the Glen to the nearby Kirkmichael station, which was beyond the viaduct.

John Snell / ColourRail

Below: In August 1964, No 5 *Mona* approaches Kirkmichael with a Douglas to Ramsey service that had split at Peel. The line had cut in from the coast at this point. The latter days of normal operation saw two coaches as more than enough for the traffic that was expected. *Mona* looks very smart and her dome is well polished, illustrating the 'pride in the job' that existed on the railway.

D J Mitchell / ColourRail

Above: Railcars Nos 20 and 19, with a van in between, prepare to leave Castletown for Port Erin in April 1965. It was the Port Erin line that gave the railcars adhesion troubles, as each one had to pull the eleven and a half tons of the other. Their Gardner diesel engines could not both be controlled from the leading cab. Because of this, they performed most of their duties on the Peel and Ramsey routes.

ColourRail

Below: No 16 *Mannin* stands outside the locomotive shed at Port Erin on the 8 September 1962 awaiting servicing by her crew. She was ordered specially for the Port Erin line and its heavy grades. The shed was rebuilt in 1908, complete with water tower.

ColourRail

ISLE OF MAN RAILWAY

NOTICE—The hours or times stated in the Company's Time Tables, Books, Bills and Notices are appointed as those at which it is intended so far as circumstances will permit, that the trains shall depart from and arrive at the several Stations, but their departure or arrival at the times stated is not guaranteed, nor will the Company under any circumstances be held responsible for delay or detention, however occasioned, or any consequences arising therefrom. The right to stop the trains at any station on the lines although not marked as a stopping Station, and to alter or suspend the running of any of the trains, is reserved.

This Time Table will Not Operate on Any Day that may require a Special Time Table.

Time Table for Tuesday, 6th July, 1965, and until further notice

DOUGLAS—PORT ERIN LINE — WEEKDAYS

To PORT ERIN

Stations	6	8	10	12	14	16
DOUGLAS Dep.	10 0	10 30	11 45	2 15	3 40	5 25
Port Soderick ,,	...	10 41	11 56	2 26	R	5 36
Ballasalla ,,	...	10 57	12 12	2 42	4 7	5 52
Castletown ,,	10 33	11 3	12 18	2 48	4 13	5 58
Colby ,,	10 42	R	R	R	4 21	R
Port St. Mary ,,	10 49	11 18	12 33	3 3	4 28	6 13
PORT ERIN Arr.	10 51	11 20	12 35	3 5	4 30	6 15

16 — Runs from 19th July to 21st August

To DOUGLAS

Stations	B	7	9	13	15	17	19
PORT ERIN Dep.	7 40	10 35	11 50	2 15	3 45	4 10	5 30
Port St. Mary ,,	7 35	10 38	11 53	2 18		4 15	5 33
Colby ,,	7 49	10 43	11 58	2 23		4 20	5 38
Castletown ,,	8 1	10 52	12 7	2 32		4 29	5 47
Ballasalla ,,	8 9	10 58	12 13	2 41	4 6	4 36	5 53
Port Soderick ,,	...	R	12 30	R		4 53	6 10
DOUGLAS Arr.	8 35	11 25	12 40	3 10	4 33	5 5	6 20

19 — Runs from 19th July to 21st August

DOUGLAS—PEEL and RAMSEY LINES — WEEKDAYS

To PEEL AND RAMSEY

Stations	B	6	8	10	12	14	16	B
DOUGLAS Dep.		10 0	10 25		12 0	2 10	3 25	4 15
Crosby ,,		R	R		12 14	R	R	
St. John's Arr.		10 23	10 48		12 23	2 33	3 48	CV
St. John's Dep.		10 26		10 51	12 26	2 36	3 51	
PEEL Arr.		10 35		11 0	12 35	2 45	4 0	
St. John's Dep.			10 53			2 38		
Kirk Michael ,,	8 0		11 14			2 59		5 0
Ballaugh ,,	8 8		11 22			3 7		5 9
Sulby Glen ,,	8 15		11 28			3 13		5 15
Sulby Bridge ,,	8 17		11 31			3 16		5 17
RAMSEY Arr.	8 30		11 40			3 25		5 30

To DOUGLAS

Stations	B	B	B	7	9	11	15	17	19
RAMSEY Dep.		7 20				1 45			4 0
Sulby Bridge ,,		7 30				1 55			4 10
Sulby Glen ,,		7 33				1 58			4 13
Ballaugh ,,		7 41				2 4			4 19
Kirk Michael ,,		7 50				2 12			4 27
St. John's Arr.		CV				2 32			4 47
PEEL Dep.	7 25		8 5	10 40	11 15	2 25	3 40	4 25	
St. John's Arr.	7 34		8 14	10 49	11 24	2 34	3 49	4 34	
St. John's Dep.	7 34		8 16		11 27	2 37	3 52	4 37	4 52
Crosby ,,	7 47	8 20	8 26		11 37	2 47	4 2	4 47	5 2
DOUGLAS Arr.	8 0	8 35	8 40		11 50	3 0	4 15	5 0	5 15

19 — Runs 5 mins. later to 21 July

B — Bus. R — Request Stop.
CV—Via Cronk-y-Voddy and Ballacraine.

See also bus time table for connections with steamers.

SUNDAY MORNINGS—TRAINS TO KIRK BRADDAN—Douglas depart from 10-10 a.m., returning after the Open-air Church Service.

MANXLAND'S MOST CHARMING RESORTS AND LOVELIEST GLENS
are along the routes served by the
STEAM RAILWAY

SPECIAL DAY EXCURSION AND RUNABOUT TICKETS

IT COSTS SO LITTLE TO SEE THE ISLAND BY TRAIN!

DO NOT FAIL TO VISIT——
GLEN WYLLIN (Kirk Michael Station)
A beautiful Glen on the Western Shore. BOATING LAKE, CHILDREN'S PLAYGROUND. Luncheons, Teas, Snacks at reasonable charges.

Douglas. 　　　　　　　　　　　　　　　　　E. R. CAIN, Secretary.

Island Development Co. Ltd

14

ISLE OF MAN STEAM LOCOMOTIVES

No	Name	Built	Works	No	Notes
1	Sutherland	1873	Beyer Peacock	1253	
2	Derby	1873	Beyer Peacock	1254	Dismantled 1951
3	Pender	1873	Beyer Peacock	1255	
4	Loch	1874	Beyer Peacock	1416	
5	Mona	1874	Beyer Peacock	1417	
6	Peveril	1875	Beyer Peacock	1524	
7	Tynwald	1880	Beyer Peacock	2038	Dismantled 1945
8	Fenella	1894	Beyer Peacock	3610	
9	Douglas	1896	Beyer Peacock	3815	
10	G H Wood	1905	Beyer Peacock	4662	
11	Maitland	1905	Beyer Peacock	4663	
12	Hutchinson	1908	Beyer Peacock	5126	
13	Kissack	1910	Beyer Peacock	5382	
14	Thornhill	1880	Beyer Peacock	2028	Ex-MNR No 3, 1905 (renumbered 1918)
15	Caledonia	1885	Dubs	2178	Ex-MNR No 4, 1905 (renumbered 1922), 0-6-0T
(16	Ramsey)	1879	Sharp Stewart	2885	Ex-MNR No 1, 1905 (scr 1922, IOMR number never carried)
16	Mannin	1926	Beyer Peacock	6296	
(17	Northern)	1879	Sharp Stewart	2886	Ex-MNR No 1, 1905 (scr 1922, IOMR number never carried)

Apart from 0-6-0T No 15, all locomotives were 2-4-0Ts.

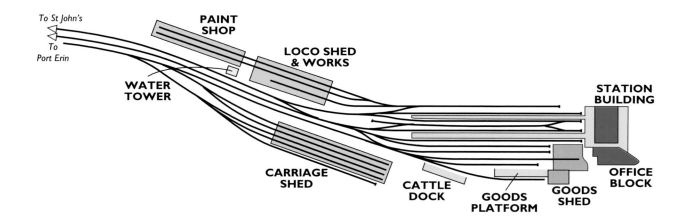

PAINT SHOP

LOCO SHED & WORKS

To St John's

To Port Erin

WATER TOWER

STATION BUILDING

CARRIAGE SHED

CATTLE DOCK

GOODS PLATFORM

GOODS SHED

OFFICE BLOCK

— Douglas —

Below: Douglas station front is seen during the second year of 'The Ailsa Era' on 2 July 1968. The first station at Douglas was a timber structure, but it was replaced in 1892 by the current building of Ruabon red bricks (see below). At the same time, the whole platform area and goods shed was upgraded, complete with a four road carriage shed.

ColourRail

Above: Douglas goods depot is seen in March 1966, during the year the railway was closed, with a number of 'M' wagons and a 'G' van being loaded and unloaded. Lorry No 21 is in attendance. The IMR had a fleet of lorries for collection and delivery services to and from station forwarding points.

D J Mitchell / ColourRail

Below: Lorry No 24, which appears to be carrying a load of trunks, stands outside Douglas goods shed in August 1964. The staff are checking the delivery address labels and ensuring correct stowage. Through the shed, another lorry and the signalbox, and signals, controlling the station throat can be seen.

D J Mitchell / ColourRail

Above: No 5 *Mona* waits for departure time at Douglas with the 9.45am to Ramsey on 20 April 1957. Coach F13, of 1894 vintage, is immediately behind the locomotive. The raised platforms and awnings were added by 1909, and a WC block opened in 1913!

D J Mitchell / ColourRail

Below: No 3 *Pender* is seen on the same day, leaving with a Peel service. The length of the platform awnings is well illustrated (sadly demolished in 1980, together with the original Port Erin line platforms).

ColourRail

Above: No 3 *Pender* makes a smart departure from Douglas with a Peel train in 1956. On shed is No 12 *Hutchinson*, being prepared for a tube clean, together with the omni-present line of spare wheel sets. The two locomotives make interesting comparison, *Hutchinson* having a straighter fronted smokebox with larger water tanks. Visible between the two locomotives is a vintage shovel for moving piles of coal, made by Priestmans.

ColourRail

Below: No 5 *Mona* moves empty stock from the platforms at Douglas, following an arrival from Peel and Ramsey on 8 September 1962. No 16 *Mannin* stands in the centre run-round road and takes water, prior to moving towards the sheds. Carriages are stabled to the right of the locomotives, next to the goods shed. Sadly most of this area is now a car and bus park.

ColourRail

Above: Nos 16 and 12 pull crisply out of Douglas with a Peel and Ramsey service in 1960. To the left of the locomotives are the carriage sheds and an excellent view of the signal box is afforded from this position. The box was built by Dutton & Co of Worcester in 1892 and contained a 36 lever frame.

ColourRail

Below: Looking back from the box gives a fine view of No 10 *G H Wood* leaving Douglas with the 2.00pm to Port Erin on 20 April 1957. To the right the small goods shed can be seen, together with a variety of wagons including 'G' and 'M' types.

ColourRail

Above: A view from the west end of Douglas station shows the locomotive servicing area and sheds. Large piles of coal are evident, as are three locomotives — Nos 11, 13 and 14. Two classic signals, so much a feature of Douglas station, guard the platform exits. The 'S' on the right hand arm allowed a shunting movement to pull forward under the control of the signalman. The date is 18 August 1960.

Peter Gray / ColourRail

Below: A rare scene inside the locomotive shed at Douglas on 3 June 1964. Locomotives Nos 1 *Sutherland* and 14 *Thornhill* await servicing. The inspection pits between the rails can be seen as well as some re-railing jacks. It is good news that No 1 has been restored to full working order after many years in storage.

ColourRail

Above: A Ramsey train gets underway from Douglas, with No 5 *Mona* in charge, on 20 April 1957. The fine main bracket signal is well illustrated as well as the long carriage shed roads to the right.

ColourRail

— Douglas to St John's —

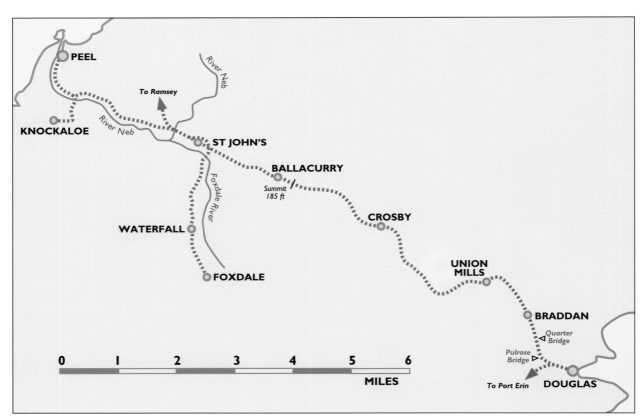

Above: The approach to Douglas is illustrated on 1 May 1969 with the two main lines — the left hand one from St John's and the right from Port Erin — coming together at this point. The fine signals were outer homes which gave an early indication of the main signals in the distance. A locomotive boiler is seen dumped on a flat wagon in the adjoining siding. Only the Port Erin line operated in 1969 (the right hand track here), the Peel and Ramsey lines having closed in September 1968. *ColourRail*

Below: No 8 *Fenella* gets away from Douglas with a service for Peel in 1962. A superb distant signal guards the approach. In the distance the bracket home signal can be seen, whose aspects were repeated on the main inner home signals that were situated at Douglas station. *ColourRail*

Above: No 13 *Kissack* approaches Pulrose Bridge with a Ramsey train in 1960. The bridge replaced a former level crossing. There was once a siding here that was used by trains to bring spoil from the mines at Foxdale to construct the King George V playing fields in the 1930s.

ColourRail

Below: A small distance further on comes Quarter Bridge and, in May 1965, railcars 19 and 20 pass by with a service to Peel. There was a gated crossing here, complete with a crossing keeper's house, as there was no station to provide such staff. A small halt was used for a brief time in the 1920s. The railcars came from the County Donegal Railway in 1961, having been supplied in 1950 and 1951 respectively by Walker Bros of Wigan. Each is powered by a 6LW Gardner diesel engine which is connected to an 0-4-0 power bogie with connecting rods. The coach part is articulated onto the power bogie and was built at the Great Northern Railway's works at Dundalk. No 19 ran 371,096 miles and No 20, 348,951 on the CDR before the sale to the IOMR.

D J Mitchell / ColourRail

Above: The railcars are seen again, this time at Braddan, along with No 12 which has a special for Douglas. Braddan was a venue for open air church services, this being such an occasion on 2 August 1964. No 12 has two trains from Douglas coupled together to form the return working.

D J Mitchell / ColourRail

Below: No 12 *Hutchinson* passes Union Mills with a Bradden special service for Douglas in 1962. Union Mills served the Douglas racecourse, The Union Corn and Woollen Mills (hence the name), plus a quarry. Union Mills was set up by William Kelly in the early 19th Century and the village took its name from it. Originally the station was no more than a wooden hut, trains being controlled by the station master. However, this did not prove satisfactory as, on the twelfth day of services, a stationary passenger train was hit by a contractor's ballast train due to a signalling error. A passing loop, platform and siding were added in 1906-7. This was important as it allowed extra operating room for the express service from Ramsey to Douglas.

John Adams / ColourRail

Above: No 8 *Fenella* passes Union Mills with a lengthy train for Ramsey on 1 August 1964. Note the raised platform on one side only.

D J Mitchell / ColourRail

Below: No 12 *Hutchinson* runs round the stock of a Braddan church special at Union Mills on 2 August 1964. The locomotive has already brought in one train from Douglas which it has run round and propelled towards Crosby. It then returned to Douglas to pick up the next train which it is running round here. The two trains were then joined up and the complete train taken back to Douglas. The station buildings are well illustrated and just behind the locomotive is the competition — the bridge carrying the Douglas to Peel main road.

D J Mitchell / ColourRail

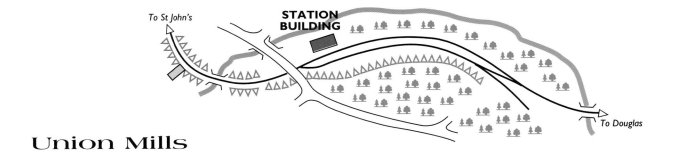

Union Mills

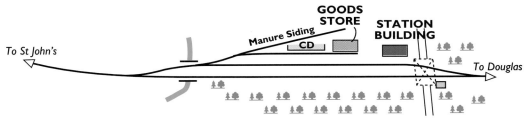

Crosby

Below: No 8 *Fenella* arrives at Crosby with the 10.25am Douglas to Ramsey on 3 August 1964. The train is banked by No 1 *Sutherland*, which went as far as the climb from St John's to St Germain's. Crosby originally had a small wooden station like that at Santon on the Port Erin line. This was rebuilt in 1910. A passing loop here was extended in 1910, complete with manure siding and cattle handling facilities. Sadly, after closure, the buildings were demolished and the site razed.

D J Mitchell / ColourRail

Above: No 15 *Caledonia* gets ready to leave Crosby on 2 June 1968 with an IMR Supporters Special train for St John's. She is carrying her former 'Manx Northern' livery following a repaint from 'Ailsa Green', the livery she had carried when breaking the tape on re-opening day on 3 June 1967. Owing to locomotive shortages, she had been rostered to work the south line the year before but this had not proved a success and she was stored, following closure, in the carriage sheds at St John's. This occasion was the last time she took a train out, until her recent rebuild.

D J Mitchell / ColourRail

Below: From Crosby to St John's the line climbed at a maximum of 1 in 130 to the summit at Ballacurry, 185ft above sea level. The approach to St John's took the line under the Foxdale branch and No 8 *Fenella*, on a Ramsey train, is just about to pass under the bridge that carried it. To the right of the main line is a siding to a ballast pit. The date is April 1956.

John Snell / ColourRail

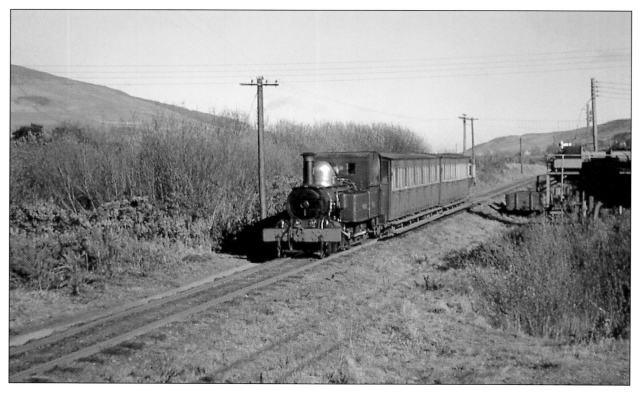

Above: Looking at St John's from the Foxdale branch bridge on 4 July 1968. A train takes the junction for Peel, the right hand route being the start of the section to Ramsey. In the distance the service from Peel approaches to cross the arrival from Douglas. The carriage shed is visible through the trees

D J Mitchell / ColourRail

— St John's —

St John's is worth a section on its own having gained the status of an important junction with the arrival of the Manx Northern line from Ramsey in 1879 and the Foxdale line in 1886. The MNR originally had its own station, west of the level crossing, and the tracks ran parallel towards the west. Following total closure of the northern routes from 1968, a certain amount of rolling stock was stored here in the carriage shed. The shed and its contents were, amazingly, included in the sale of the northern lines to the scrap merchants in 1973. A fire on 10 July 1975 damaged some of what was left, but some of the undamaged stock was preserved, including some MNR six-wheeled coaches. Another fire finally destroyed the shed in 1976. St John's saw considerable activities on Tynwald Day and trains ran from all destinations for the ceremonies.

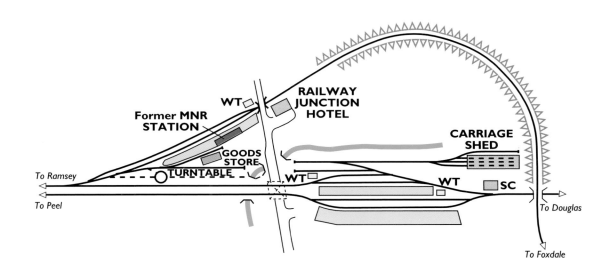

Above: Looking toward Douglas from St John's in April 1956 we see the line straddled by the branch line to Foxdale. The upper arm of the signal controlled the Peel route and the lower was for Ramsey. Just beyond the signal, the line split for the two destinations.

John Snell / ColourRail

Below: No 6 has arrived at St John's with the Ramsey portion of a combined train for Ramsey and Peel from Douglas. Splitting these trains was a complicated affair.

The train would halt at the aforementioned home signal and the pilot locomotive would then run forward to take water, the signalman controlling this movement with a white flag. The train engine would then draw in with the Peel train, leaving the Ramsey portion to be pulled in by the pilot locomotive or a locomotive that had previously brought in a Ramsey service. The aim was to return locomotives to their own sheds, as well as to send trains to the right place.

Brian Cocksey / ColourRail

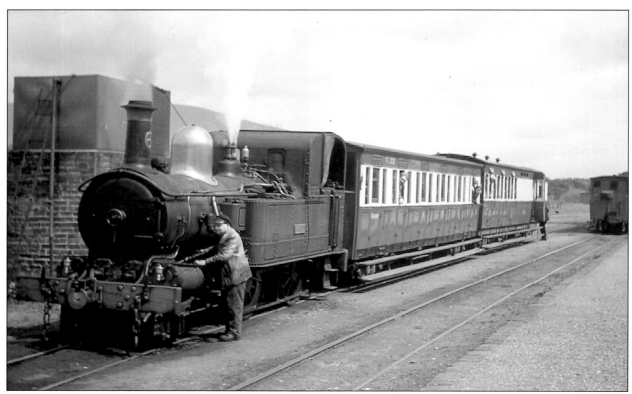

Above: No 5 *Mona* has just arrived at St John's with a train from Peel in August 1960. The station name-board advises passengers to change for Ramsey; the other side advises of a change for Peel. In the background stands one of the 'Empress' full brakes, probably in use as an ambulance coach for the TT races.

ColourRail

Below: St John's at a busy moment on 18 August 1960 sees No 8 arriving on the 10.00am from Ramsey to Douglas and crossing No 5 with the 10.25am Douglas to Ramsey. No 8's driver has just taken the tablet for the Douglas route. The parallel single lines, left to Peel, right to Ramsey, can be seen stretching away into the distance.

Peter Gray / ColourRail

Above: No 8 blows off impatiently while awaiting departure for Peel in August 1957. Although there was a footbridge at St John's, until 1945, most passengers simply walked across the tracks to change trains.

ColourRail

Below: A good view of the level crossing gates at St John's on 20 April 1957, with No 14 *Thornhill* making a spirited departure for Ramsey. The station master stands by the gate, which is half closed across the Peel line. Simultaneous departures for Peel and Ramsey were discouraged to prevent racing — however this did happen from time to time!

ColourRail

Above: The Ramsey line climbed above the Peel line in order to gain height for the climb to St Germain's, before veering away north west just past a bridge over the River Neb. No 5 *Mona* is shortly to cross the bridge with its Ramsey train in 1962.

John Adams / ColourRail

Below: No 16 *Mannin* heads for St John's and Douglas with a train from Peel in 1962 and is about to commence running parallel with the Ramsey route.

John Adams / ColourRail

Below: A panoramic view that on closer inspection reveals two trains. The lines to Peel (on the right) and Ramsey (on the left) are well illustrated by the two trains that have 'raced' each other from St John's, No 8 *Fenella* heading the Ramsey portion and No 5 *Mona* heading the Peel portion of the 3.25pm from Douglas on 19 August 1960.

ColourRail

— The Foxdale Line —

Above: The first station on the Foxdale line was at Waterfall, which actually served the hamlet of Lower Foxdale. The station building originally stood at St John's. Amazingly the track was still down in May 1960 when this photograph was taken, looking towards St John's.

D J Mitchell / ColourRail

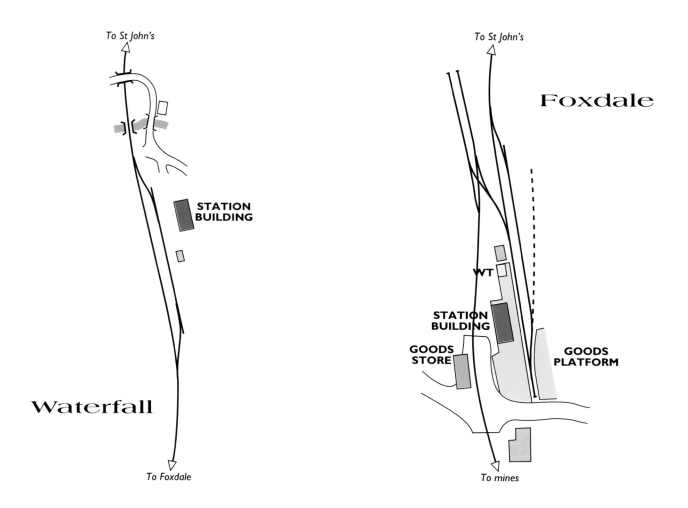

To St John's

To St John's

Foxdale

STATION BUILDING

WT

STATION BUILDING

GOODS STORE

GOODS PLATFORM

Waterfall

To Foxdale

To mines

Below: Despite mining ceasing in 1911 and passenger services in 1943, track remained in situ at Foxdale in July 1961. Two freight services ran as late as January 1960. The line to the mines ran to the right of the building and the rubble on the left was spoil from the workings. Large quantities of this spoil was used for constructing airfield runways during the war and playing fields in Douglas. Originally the Manx Northern planned an extension from Foxdale to Ballasalla, but this came to nought.

John Snell / ColourRail

— Peel —

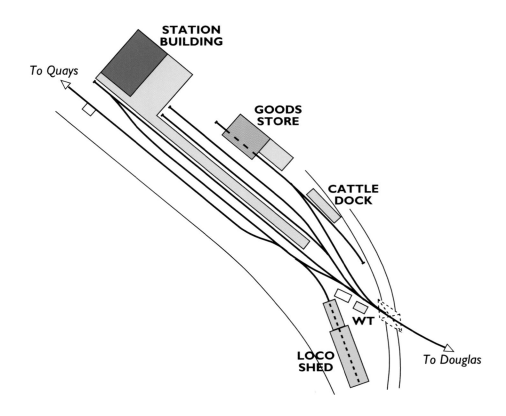

Below: Running close to the River Neb the line terminated next to the quayside at Peel. This view, taken from Corrins Hill, illustrates the situation well. The locomotive shed can be seen bottom right, as can two trains. No 5 *Mona* is arriving on the 3.25pm from Douglas and No 13 *Kissack* waits to leave with the 4.30pm to Douglas on 18 August 1960.

Peter Gray / ColourRail

Above: Peel shed on the Ailsa re-opening day of 3 June 1967. No 8 *Fenella* is serviced, after working one of the specials from Douglas. The level crossing gates across Mill Road are open for another train and a feeling of optimism for the future abounds. The locomotive sports her new coat of 'Ailsa green' and carries the special headcode carried on re-opening day. The locomotive shed was the only building demolished following closure.

ColourRail

Below: Looking back at Peel station, with No 8 *Fenella* waiting to leave on a train for Douglas in 1962. The driver is sitting on the platform edge in a manner that would no doubt cause much difficulty with today's Health and Safety regulations! The goods shed now houses the replica longboat *Odin's Raven* and the station buildings have survived as the *House of Mananan* (a heritage centre).

John Adams / ColourRail

Above: In 1968 three M wagons were converted to take 3,500 gallon tanks to carry oil by rail from Peel to Ramsey, on a thrice weekly basis (see also page 70). From Ramsey they ran back to Milntown Power Station, where a new siding was constructed. The venture started on 13 August 1968 and lasted until 29 April 1969. Here No 12 *Hutchinson* is seen picking up the tanks at Peel Power Station in August 1968.

ColourRail

Below: Railcars Nos 20 and 19 wait to leave Peel with a Douglas service in 1967. The relatively flat run to Peel suited the railcars better than the Port Erin line, given that the leading car had to haul the other one 'dead'. However, the cars are piped so that the brakes on both can be operated from the leading car.

D J Mitchell / ColourRail

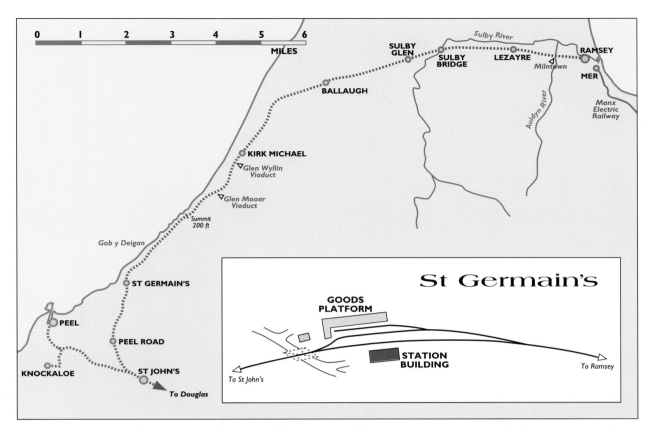

Below: No 14 *Thornhill* is seen on MNR home territory, at St Germain's, with a Ramsey service on 4 June 1960. The station did not feature in timetables, from 1961, but trains still called there. The building, of red sandstone, is pure MNR design. The station once saw much sand traffic for building purposes — hence the loading dock — and also sported a loop, which was lifted, reinstated in 1926, only to be lifted again in 1954.

Chris Gammell / ColourRail

Above: The County Donegal railcars are seen near Lady Port with a service from Peel to Ramsey in August 1967. No 20 is leading — note that she has more windows with top vents than her sister No 19, behind. Those who are CDR experts will also notice that the little used roof racks have also been removed.

D J Mitchell / ColourRail

Below: No 8 *Fenella* returns to Douglas with a special train that has left Ramsey at 9.45am on 3 June 1968 and runs through Gob-y-Deigan, illustrating what a spectacular run the Ramsey line was. It was this section of line that was washed away by floods, caused by heavy rainfall, in April 1889. In 1968 increased losses caused the premature ending of the summer season, the Ramsey line closing on 6 September and Peel and Port Erin on the following day. The first two were not to re-open.

ColourRail

Above: No 5 *Mona* crosses Glen Mooar viaduct with a train for Ramsey in 1961. The Irish Sea is in the background as the photographer looks back towards Gob-y-Deigan.

ColourRail

Below: Railcars Nos 19 (left) and 20 cross Glen Wyllin viaduct with a Ramsey train in August 1964. The tourist development is well illustrated here, with the bowling greens being enjoyed by some potential customers. One wonders if they had travelled by train and walked down from Kirkmichael!

ColourRail

Above: No 8 *Fenella* arrives at Kirkmichael with the 10.25am Douglas to Ramsey on 1 August 1964. She is just about to cross the level crossing and enter the main loop where some trains terminated for Glen Wyllin. The footpath to the Glen can be seen in the foreground. *Fenella* was the regular Ramsey line locomotive for many years.

D J Mitchell / ColourRail

Below: Inside the station buildings at Kirkmichael on 19 August 1960 was a remarkable display of period posters, for both the railway and various other operators, including the famous White Star shipping line of *Titanic* fame. Even in 1960, ocean liners were the preferred way to travel to the United States and Canada. 50p a week for a 'Run About' ticket seems remarkable value today.

Peter Gray / ColourRail

Above: Railcars 19 and 20 are seen at Kirkmichael's MNR station with a Ramsey service on 1 August 1964. The expected savings that the diesels were expected to make did not prove great enough to stem the losses that mounted from the off-peak season services, and the Ramsey winter services were replaced by buses from 1961. By 1965 the whole network was to close in the winter. No passenger services operated in 1966.

D J Mitchell / ColourRail

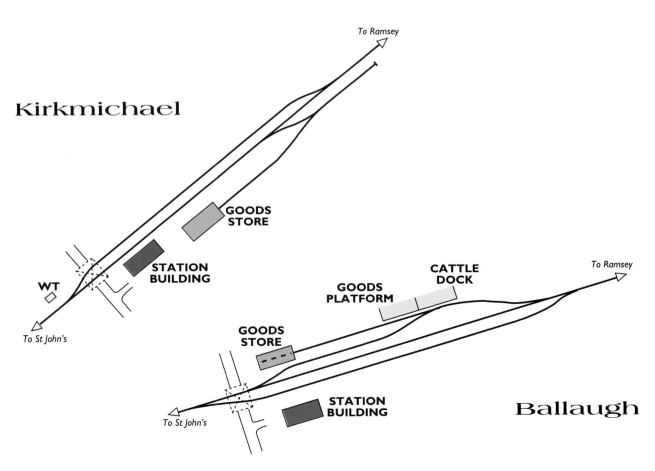

Kirkmichael

To Ramsey

GOODS STORE

STATION BUILDING

WT

To St John's

GOODS PLATFORM

CATTLE DOCK

To Ramsey

GOODS STORE

STATION BUILDING

To St John's

Ballaugh

Above: No 8 *Fenella* and No 10 *G H Wood* cross at Ballaugh in August 1967. The track is still recovering from the lack of use the previous year and is overgrown with grass. Ballaugh had a shorter passing loop than Kirkmichael but occasionally locomotives were changed here.

A M Davies / ColourRail

Below: No 8 *Fenella* waits for the off at Ballaugh with the 10.25am Douglas to Ramsey on 3 August 1964. From Ballaugh the line dipped through Coolibane up to a summit at Sulby Glen, the last summit before Ramsey.

D J Mitchell / ColourRail

Above: No 11 *Maitland* leaves Sulby Glen with a St John's service in July 1967. The station had a short platform with an awning that was part of the station building. The building replaced a small crossing lodge that was built in 1880 but demolished in 1910, when the current structure replaced it. The station also had sidings for cattle and general goods.

D J Mitchell / ColourRail

Below: No 8 *Fenella* arrives at Sulby Glen with a Ramsey service on 1 August 1964. The canopy is shown to good effect, as is part of the level crossing gate.

D J Mitchell / ColourRail

CATTLE DOCK GOODS PLATFORM STATION BUILDING

To St John's   To Ramsey

Sulby Glen

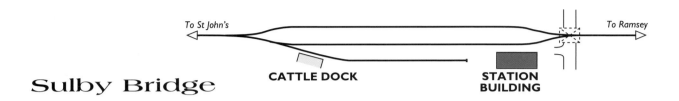

Sulby Bridge

To St John's   To Ramsey

CATTLE DOCK   STATION BUILDING

STATION BUILDING

To St John's   To Ramsey

Lezayre

Below: No 10 *G H Wood* calls at Sulby Bridge with the 10.47am St John's to Ramsey on 3 June 1968. Sulby Bridge was slightly closer to the village but travellers preferred to use Sulby Glen, which had more station facilities, as can be seen from the photograph. There was a loop here for crossing trains, although Ballaugh saw more use.

ColourRail

Above: The last stop before Ramsey was Lezayre, a building being put up here in 1880. The nearby Ballakillingan Estate encouraged the railway to construct a siding in 1884. Lezayre was like St Germain's and Santon, vanishing from the timetable before trains 'ceased to call' from 1967. However No 5 *Mona* is seen pausing there in July 1967.

D J Mitchell / ColourRail

Below: No 5 *Mona* makes a fine sight on arrival at Ramsey from St John's in 1962. The run round loop is behind the locomotive with the carriage shed in the background. On the other side of the island platform was a bay platform.

John Adams / ColourRail

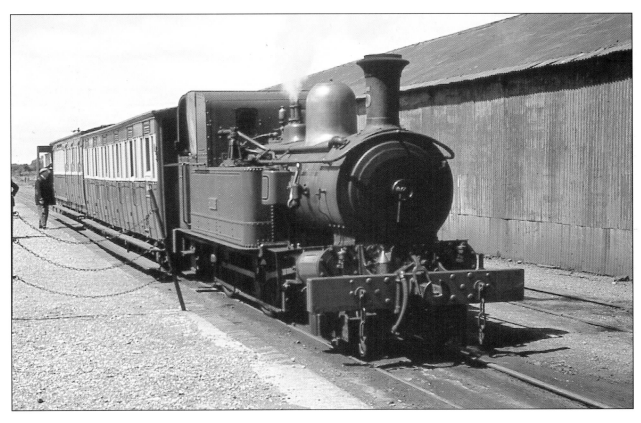

— Ramsey —

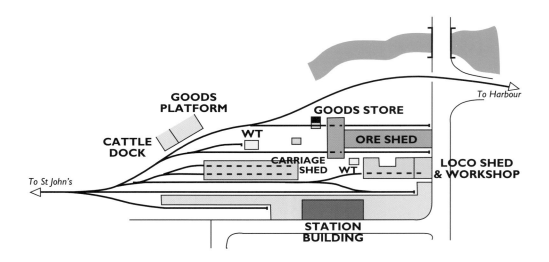

Below: Ramsey had a large station area, equipped with passenger facilities and a carriage shed. There was a locomotive shed (extended to take No 4 *Caledonia*), goods sidings and a goods shed. All this was due to the importance placed on Ramsey as the terminus of the MNR. No 14 *Thornhill* (ex-MNR No 3) runs round her train at Ramsey on 23 April 1957 to prepare to return to St John's.

ColourRail

Above: No 14 waits to leave Ramsey with the St John's and Douglas train on 23 April 1957. This is a classic IOMR mixed train — freight only services were seldom run. The carriage shed can be seen on the left with the station buildings shown on the right. The branch line to Ramsey harbour was a key source of traffic to and from Foxdale mines, along with other general merchandise and this ran over to the northern side of the site behind the sheds, being lifted in 1956. *ColourRail*

Below: The northern side of the site is seen in this view as No 10 *G H Wood* shunts a wagon of tomatoes at Ramsey in August 1967. The one time link to Ramsey harbour ran off to the through gate to the right of the wagon.

D J Mitchell / ColourRail

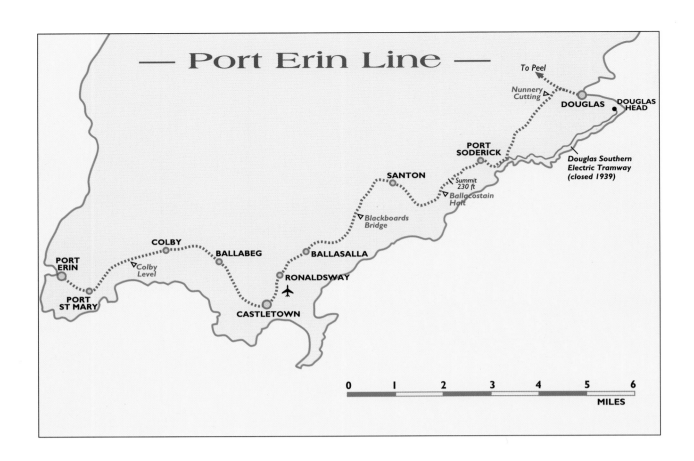

Port Erin Line

Port Soderick

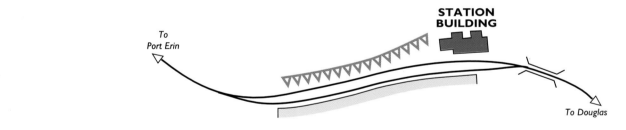

Santon

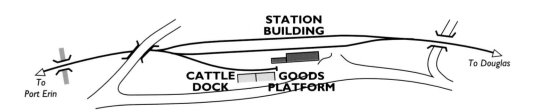

Above: No 5 *Mona* crosses a Douglas train at Port Soderick in July 1967. The original small station was rebuilt in 1896 and the impressive structure behind the train was the result. A passing loop had also been added in 1894. Port Soderick attracted many tourists in the years before the First World War, becoming subject to competition from the Douglas Southern Electric tramway although, such was demand, both railways coped. Heavy IOMR trains were banked from Douglas through Nunnery up 1:70 / 1:63 gradients to Port Soderick, the banker then returning light to Douglas.

D J Mitchell / ColourRail

Below: A train for Douglas arrives at Santon in 1962 headed by No 12 *Hutchinson*. In 1910, a siding for cattle and manure traffic was built here. On 3 March 1913, a carriage was derailed on the loop points where someone placed a stone in the blades. The stationmaster, who apparently had not made an inspection, was given the blame. Two years later, there was a fire at the station. At this time, Santon was an unstaffed halt — not even appearing in the timetables in some instances. The photographer is standing right next to the station buildings. One of these is a store shed from a converted 'E' body.

John Adams / ColourRail

Above: No 10 *G H Wood* approaches Santon from Port Erin in 1962. The train is about to enter the station and has two vans in tow for general merchandise. The home signal controlled the approach to the station.

John Adams / ColourRail

Below: Ballasalla station is situated roughly half way between Douglas and Port Erin. No 16 *Mannin* arrives on 18 August 1960 with the 11.45am Douglas to Port Erin service. The loop here dates back to 1874. The train will have descended towards Ballasalla down a 1:80 gradient, this necessitating Up trains for Douglas, of over eight coaches, to be banked, or worked in separate portions. No 16 would more than likely take water here, having worked hard on the climb from Douglas.

Peter Gray / ColourRail

Above: No 10 *G H Wood* stands at Ballasalla on 20 April 1957 with a Down Port Erin service. The goods sidings are connected to the Up loop and were improved in 1893, with a goods shed being added in 1920. A cattle dock was also added to cope with business for Ballasalla market.

ColourRail

Below: Ronaldsway Halt was opened in 1967 to serve the airport. The halt was one of the initiatives of the Ailsa era but facilities were sparse, as can be seen from the photograph. A train for Port Erin, headed by No 5 *Mona*, approaches in July 1967.

D J Mitchell / ColourRail

Ballasalla

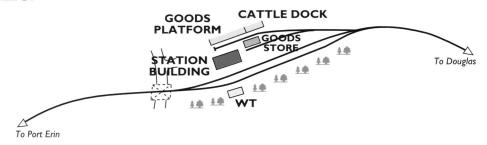

Castletown

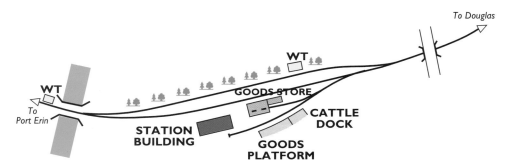

Below: No 6 *Peveril* stands at Castletown with a Port Erin service in August 1957. Lorry No 2 is prepared to receive goods from another train for collection and delivery. Watering facilities were available in both directions. Castletown was the original proposed terminus and a more substantial building was added, to replace the original 1881 station, in 1902. Wagons off Down passenger trains were fly shunted into the sidings as the train was moving.

ColourRail

Above: Ballabeg Halt served a hamlet and in the period covered by this book little stopped there. It is seen in March 1966 during the year, prior to Ailsa, that the railway was closed. Like other smaller stations it appeared and disappeared from timetables. Fortunately, Ballabeg has now been restored and re-opened.

D J Mitchell / ColourRail

Below: No 10 *G H Wood* crosses No 11 *Maitland* on a Down Port Erin train at Colby, on 31 July 1964. Colby was similar to Ballasalla in layout and construction, and was the highest point between Castletown and Port Erin. Colby's siding (with a cattle dock) faced Douglas and a loop was put in in 1907. The station building came from Braddan and, like most IOMR stations, had no platforms.

D J Mitchell / ColourRail

Colby

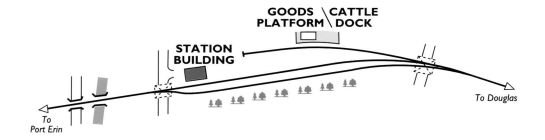

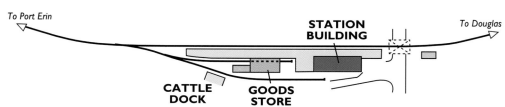

Port St Mary

Below: The last stop before Port Erin was Port St Mary. No 11 *Maitland* pulls away with the 10.10am Douglas to Port Erin train on 4 August 1964. The station building was constructed in the same brick as Douglas and a platform provided. There were sidings and a goods shed, the local gas-works bringing a small amount of coal traffic business for the railway

D J Mitchell / ColourRail

Above: A good overall view of Port Erin is seen from the level crossing that is crossed on arrival. The station buildings were erected in 1905, followed by a goods shed and a new locomotive shed in 1908. The goods shed is now the Port Erin Railway Museum. No 12 *Hutchinson* shunts stock on 18 August 1960, in preparation for working a train to Douglas.

Peter Gray / ColourRail

Below: No 8 *Fenella* has arrived at Port Erin on a train from Douglas on 3 August 1964. No 10 *G H Wood* has moved onto the back of the train for the return working. A good view of the close proximity of the station to the town is shown. In the years before the Second World War, when traffic was at its peak, long, double-headed, fourteen coach trains (up to thirteen per day) would bring tourists to Port Erin from Douglas.

ColourRail

Above: Railcars 20 and 19 (right) look very smart at Port Erin on 4 August 1964, as they prepare to leave for Douglas. The style of the station building is almost like a Swiss chalet and a classic Ford Anglia is parked on the platform.

D J Mitchell / ColourRail

Below: No 10 *G H Wood* at Port Erin, with lorry No 14 on 20 April 1959. The photograph illustrates the door to door service provided by the railway. However, this required a certain amount of trans-shipment between train and lorry. In the end this was one of the reasons that the railway found it difficult to compete with road carriers, who were not dependent on the arrival or departure of trains.

ColourRail

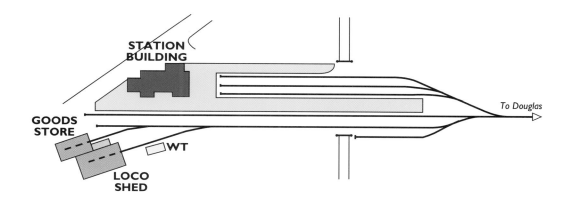

Port Erin

— Locomotives —

Below: Locomotive No 1 *Sutherland* (BP1253), was built by Beyer Peacock at Gorton Foundry in 1873. She was named after the Duke of Sutherland, who was chairman of the IOMR, and pulled a test train (formed of wagons with seats in them!) from Douglas to Peel on 1 May 1873, with the Duke on the footplate. She suffered a rather unfortunate start, as she was derailed at Peel and the train had to be rescued by the building contractor's locomotive *Mona*.

Here, *Sutherland* is seen shunting stock at Douglas on 16 July 1956. Like nearly all her sisters, *Sutherland* had 11"x 18" cylinders and weighed 19 tons. She spent many years in the Port Erin Museum but was recently restored to working order for the 125th anniversary celebrations. Locomotive No 2 *Derby* was broken up in 1951 and, unfortunately, it has proved impossible to find a colour transparency of her.

T J Edgington / ColourRail

Above: The first nine locomotives were fitted with small boilers and were standardised to allow the interchange of spare parts. No 3 *Pender* (BP 1255) was named after Sir John Pender, who was Chairman of the IOMR for seventeen years, after The Duke of Sutherland's seven year stint following opening. The same as Nos 1 & 2, No 3 is now on display as an exhibit in the Greater Manchester Museum of Science and Industry. Here she is seen waiting to depart from Peel for Douglas on 20 April 1957, with lorry No 15 in attendance.

ColourRail

Below No 4 *Loch* (BP1416) was built for the Port Erin line, with greater water capacity and coal space than Nos 1-3. She was named after the Island's Governor, Henry Brougham Loch. On 20 July 1905, No 4, with a combined Peel and Ramsey train, hit the stop blocks at Douglas and then suffered another mishap at St John's on 4 November when it ran into a stationary coach. She originally carried a smaller boiler but, on its second rebuild in 1909, she received a larger boiler, side tanks and cab. No 4 stands at Douglas with a Port Erin service on 10 August 1972. She was in service up to 1997.

ColourRail

Above: No 5 *Mona* (BP1417) was delivered with her sister No 4 in 1874 and is seen standing by the water tower and locomotive shed at Peel. She too was designed for the Port Erin line.

ColourRail

Below: No 6 *Peveril* (BP1875) was received from Beyer Peacock in 1875. She is standing at Peel with a Douglas service in 1956. She was named (along with No 8) after a character in the novel *Peveril of the Peak*, by Sir Walter Scott.

John Adams / ColourRail

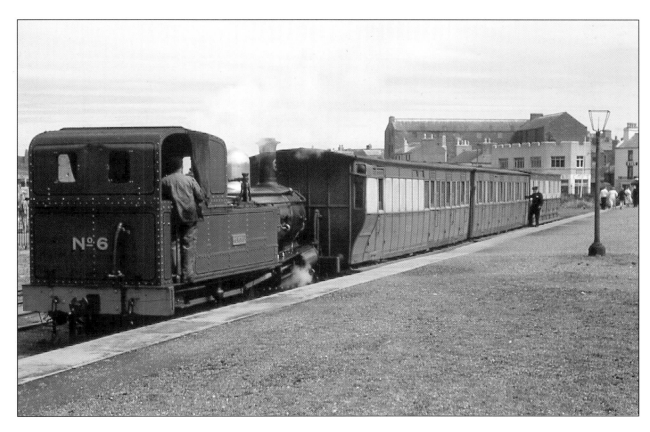

Above: No 7 *Tynwald* (BP2038) was dismantled for spares as long ago as 1946 but the frames are seen here at the back of Douglas shed. Today, they are on display at Castletown and are the property of the Isle of Man Railway and Tramway Preservation Society.

ColourRail

Below: No 8 *Fenella* (BP3610) is seen at Ramsey locomotive shed, after having arrived with a service from St John's in September 1959. No 8 was built in 1894 and is currently stored at Douglas, being owned by the Isle of Man Railway and Tramway Preservation Society. She was one of the regular Ramsey line locomotives and, like No 6, was named after a character from *Peveril of the Peak*.

W P de Beer / ColourRail

Above: No 9 *Douglas* (BP3815) stands unserviceable at Douglas in June 1970, having been placed in a siding for viewing purposes and given the 'Ailsa Green' livery. She is currently in store at Douglas.

ColourRail

Below: No 10 *G H Wood* (BP4662) arrived, with No 11, on 19 January 1905. Costing £1,405 each, they were more powerful than those previously introduced. They were ordered to provide the power for a fast service from Ramsey to Douglas, that was needed to compete with the shorter route of the Douglas to Ramsey tramway, the existing Manx Northern fleet not being suitable. They weighed 21 tons, as opposed to the 19 tons of the others. No 10 was reboilered in 1926 and fitted with Pop safety valves and a Metcalfe combination injector for the operation of vacuum brakes. Here, No 10 is seen on the southern route, at Castletown, on 31 July 1964, with a Douglas service.

D J Mitchell / ColourRail

Above: No 11 *Maitland* (BP4663) was named after Dalrymple Maitland, an IOMR board member from 1899 to 1919. She arrived, with No 10, in 1905. She makes a fine sight departing from Port Soderick with the 5.25pm Douglas to Port Erin on 4 August 1964.

D J Mitchell / ColourRail

Below: No 12 *Hutchinson* (BP5126) of 1908 is seen being serviced at Port Erin in August 1964. She was named after a railway official William A Hutchinson, who served on the Board from 1898 to 1909, and was ordered to cope with increased traffic that was developing, as the Island became a popular holiday destination.

ColourRail

Above: No 13 *Kissack* (BP5382), also named after a
company official (Edward Thomas Kissack, who served
on the Board from 1902 to 1927), arrived in 1910, the
same type as Nos 10-12. Here she is seen leaving
Douglas, and passing under Pulrose Bridge, in 1960 with
a train for Peel and Ramsey. She cost £1,283 9s 1d,
along with six guards watches for £2 15s 0d each and the
first typewriter for the head office at £23 5s 6d. The re-
railing traversing jack can clearly be seen on the right
hand tank. One hopes it will not be needed!

ColourRail

Below: No 14 *Thornhill* (BP2028) was built for the

Manx Northern Railway, as their No 3, in 1880. She was
the same type as the original IOMR fleet and weighed 19
tons. *Thornhill* was named after the home of J T Clucas,
the Chairman of the MNR. She was the last operational
locomotive to have Salter safety valves on the dome,
fitted until 1963. She is now privately preserved on the
Island. Here, she stands at St John's, with a service for
Ramsey, in April 1956. St John's had a carriage shed and
even a turntable, which was used in the main to turn
coaches, to ensure that they were consistently weathered
on both sides, after taking a battering from the west winds
on the coast line to Ramsey.

John Snell / ColourRail

Above: No 15 *Caledonia* (Dubs 2178), as an 0-6-0T, is the odd man out of the whole Isle of Man fleet. Originally designed for the projected heavy freight traffic of the Foxdale branch of the MNR, *Caledonia* was built by Dubs and Co and arrived in parts at Ramsey on 18 December 1885. She was originally MNR No 4 and her name may have had something to do with the fact that the MNR manager at the time was John Cameron, a Scot. She is an 0-6-0T, weighs 23 tons 12 cwt and was loaned to help with the construction of the Snaefell line in 1895. She was often used for snow clearing duties and on the branch to Knockaloe internment camp in 1915. She is seen at Douglas shed on 3 June 1964, complete with snow plough and admirers.

ColourRail

Below: The year 1926 saw the arrival of No 16 *Mannin* (BP 6296), which cost £3,023 12s 6d. She is a bigger locomotive than the rest of the 2-4-0Ts, having 12"x 18" cylinders, a 180lb boiler and a weight of around 23 tons. This was in order to produce a tractive effort approximately 34% greater than that of Nos 10-13. At the time, she was unique, having a square cab, whilst the other Beyer Peacocks had a rounder variety. She is seen at Douglas on a train for Peel in September 1964. Behind the locomotive is coach F13, delivered by Brown and Marshalls in 1894 and, unfortunately, burnt in the 1975 fire in St John's shed. No 16 now resides in the museum at Port Erin.

ColourRail

— Selected Coaching Stock —

Above: 'E' class vehicles were luggage and guard's vehicles. They were four-wheelers and E5 was built by the Metropolitan Railway Carriage and Wagon Works in 1876, along with E6. Dimensionally they were 16'0" x 7'0" with a height of 9'6". E5 is seen at Douglas on 20 April 1957.

ColourRail

Below: Composite bogie coach F23 was one of the bogie coaches that were delivered from 1876, initially manufactured by Brown and Marshalls. However, F23 was one of a batch made by the MRCW and was delivered in 1896. She was 35'11" x 7'0' and had a height of 9'4". The body was scrapped in 1983 and the chassis converted for weed killing and fire control.

ColourRail

Above: Brake second bogie coach F33 is seen at Douglas on 23 April 1957, waiting to form part of a Peel and Ramsey service. F33 was built by the MRCW in 1905 and was 37'0" x 7'0" with a height of 10'3''. The body has since been scrapped and the chassis is now a runner.

ColourRail

Below: Bogie brakes F27 and F28 were built by MRCW in 1897 and were known as 'Empress' vans as they were delivered in the year of Queen Victoria's Silver Jubilee. F28 is seen at St John's on 20 April 1957, in use as an ambulance coach for any injured riders in the TT races. This practice first started in 1932 and continued every year in order to get an injured rider to hospital as quickly as possible. She survives today.

ColourRail

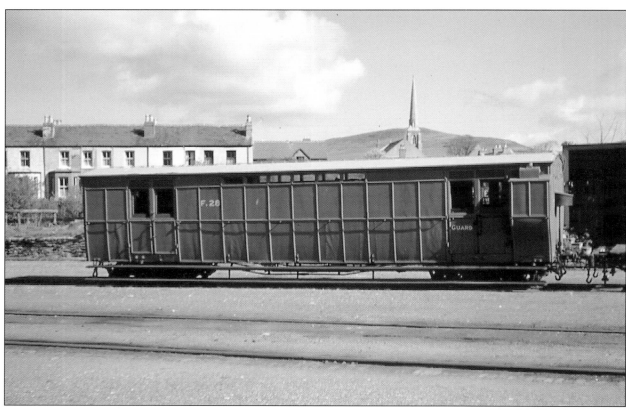

Above: Saloons F29, F30, F31 and F32 make a fine sight at Douglas on 20 April 1957. The saloons were delivered from the MRCW in 1905 and were a departure from the compartment stock used previously. They are 36'11'' x 7'0'', with a height of 10'3''. They all survive today, but Nos 31 and 32 have been fitted with new seats and tables.

ColourRail

Below: Twenty-six coaches were pairs of former four-wheelers mounted onto new bogie chassis between 1909 and 1926. F55, seen here at Peel on 20 April 1957, was converted as long ago as 1912. The small panel in the centre of the coach is where it was joined — initially some 'new' coaches ran with a gap. Many of these survive on the Island today but, unfortunately, F55 is not one of them, as the body was scrapped at St John's in 1968 and the frames were sold to the Festiniog Railway in 1974.

ColourRail

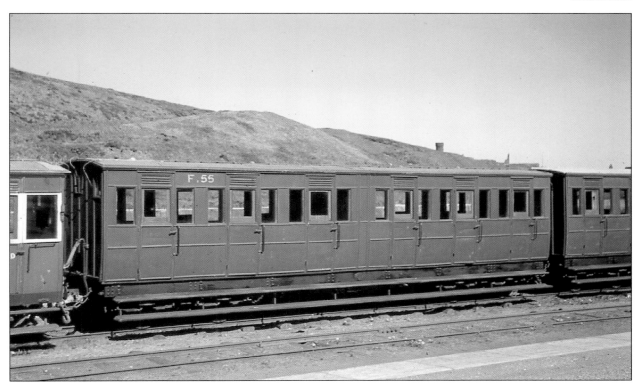

— Wagons —

Above: No 5 *Mona* is seen at Douglas with 'M' wagon No 43 on 8 September 1962. 'M' wagons were two plank and were built by a variety of companies. Ashbury built Nos 1-19 between 1877 and 1888 and these were followed by a further batch (Nos 20-27) from the MRCW in 1899. More followed from the amalgamation with the Manx Northern (Nos 28-42), the first nine coming from the Swansea Wagon Company and the rest being built by the Manx Northern at their Ramsey works between 1894 and 1898. The Foxdale Mining Company had three open wagons that were converted to 'M' wagons in 1906 becoming Nos 43-45. However they were rebuilt as 'K'

cattle wagons in 1908, being renumbered as follows: K10 (M45), K11 (M43) and K12 (M44). New Nos 43-78 were built by the MRCW between 1911 and 1926, including like for like replacements for the original 43-45.

D J Mitchell / ColourRail

Below: M61, M66 and M67 were converted into oil tankers in 1968 as part of a trial to carry oil from Peel to Milntown Power Station near Ramsey. However, with the closure of the Ramsey and Peel lines in 1969, the scheme was withdrawn and the tanks were discarded.

D J Mitchell / ColourRail

Above: No 11 *Maitland* stands at Ramsey on 25 June 1964 with two 'M' wagons and a 'G' van. The first 'G' series van was delivered in 1873. It is fitted with ventilation for carrying livestock. There were few dedicated freight-only services in the railway — these photographs illustrating the point that mixed trains were the order of the day.

ColourRail

Below: No 10 *G H Wood* leaves Douglas for Peel on a typical mixed train for Peel in September 1964. Two 'G' wagons are in the formation and would have been used to carry general merchandise. Many of the nineteen 'G' vans were broken up as freight traffic declined, many as late as 1974, but Nos 1, 12 and 19 did escape and still exist.

ColourRail

Above: Another mixed train is seen at Douglas with 'M' wagon No 52 and two 'G' class wagons that could be used for carrying cattle. There was another class of pure cattle wagons, the 'K' class, which comprised a total of twenty-six vehicles built specially for cattle on dedicated chassis and a variety of rebuilds of 'M' wagons, four-wheeled coaches and an 'E' van. The 'K' class had wider ventilators for livestock than the 'G' wagons and looked more like traditional cattle wagons. No 6 *Peveril* waits to leave with a Port Erin train in September 1956.

J H L A / ColourRail

Below: No 14 *Thornhill* has just shunted the stock for a Peel and Ramsey mixed train at Douglas on 20 April 1957. The formation includes a heavily laden 'M' wagon. *Thornhill* is awaiting the second locomotive, to double-head the train to St John's.

ColourRail